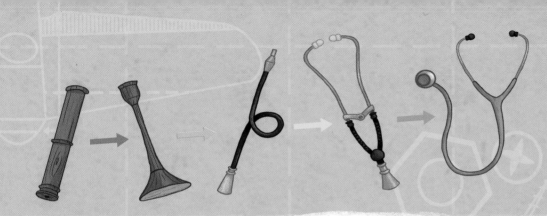

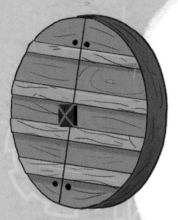

# I can be an Awesome Inventor

## Anna Claybourne

### Illustrated by Katie Kear

Dover Publications

Garden City, New York

### What is STEM?

STEM is a world-wide
initiative that aims to
cultivate an interest in
Science, Technology,
Engineering, and
Mathematics, in an effort to
promote these disciplines to
as wide a variety of students
as possible.

# Contents

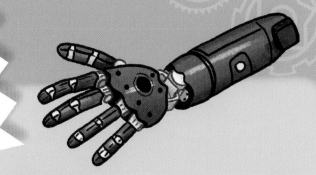

# Always Inventing!

Since prehistoric times, humans have been coming up with inventions to make life better. From stone hammers and wooden spears to boats, wheels, money, toilets, telescopes, light bulbs, and today's TVs, computers, and phones ... we're always inventing!

In this book are loads of amazing inventions, along with games, puzzles, and activities for you to try.

Animals can invent, too. Dolphins use sponges to keep their snouts safe from sharp coral while foraging for food.

But humans are the most awesome inventors of all. We have created millions of inventions, big and small!

# Activity: Catch That Mouse!

Here's a simple invention challenge to start off with. Nobody wants mice in their home, but many people don't want to harm an animal. They want a device that will trap the mouse safely inside, so it can be released later.

Can you invent a mousetrap that catches a mouse without harming it? Draw your design here to show how it would work.

**Look out!!!**

**think about:**
- how to lure the mouse inside
- how the mouse will trigger the trap to close
- how to release the mouse.

# Inventing the Wheel

The wheel is one of the most important inventions of all time. Try to imagine life without it ... you probably wouldn't get far!

Wheels are a vital part of bikes, cars, trains, and most other forms of transportation. But they're also used as parts inside all kinds of machines.

Wheels were used in Europe and Asia over 5,000 years ago. Archaeologists have found cartwheels and small wheeled toys. Their evidence also comes from ancient pictures showing wheeled vehicles.

Waterwheel

Washing machine

Ferris wheel

Well

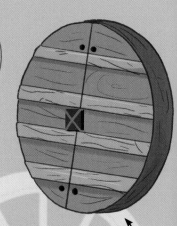
Ancient wheeled toy from Ukraine

Illustration of Sumerian wheeled cart

Old wooden cartwheel found in Slovenia

# Activity: From Logs to Wheels

No one is sure how the wheel was invented. But we do know that some ancient peoples used to move large objects, such as blocks of stone for building, by rolling them along on logs. Some experts think this led to the invention of the wheel over a series of stages.

Can you match the pictures to the text?

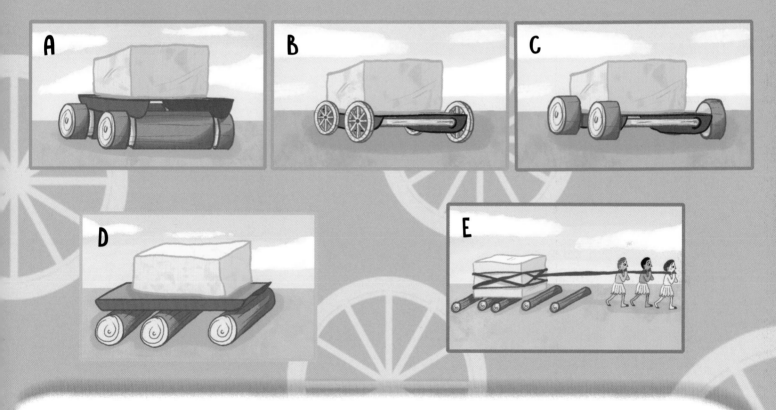

1. Object rolled along on logs. People had to keep moving logs from the back to the front, so that the object could keep going.

2. The object was placed on a flat base to make it easier to position the logs.

3. The logs were worn down by the flat base on top, creating wheel shapes at the ends.

4. People made a separate axle to go through holes in the flat base, with round wheels fixed onto the ends.

5. Wheels with spokes were invented, making the wheel lighter and stronger.

# Cogs and Gears

Gears are wheels linked with cogs, which are the teeth around the edges of the wheel. Gears are used in machines to pass on movement and change its force, angle, speed, or direction.

Here's a simple gear system that changes the direction of rotation. The cogs of the gears interlock, so that when one wheel turns, it makes the other turn, too, but in the opposite direction.

This wheel turns clockwise ...

Cogs

... making this wheel rotate the other way.

When a bigger gear turns a smaller gear, it changes the speed of rotation, making the smaller gear rotate faster.

This gear has 20 teeth

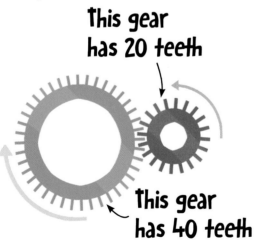

This gear has 40 teeth

When the big gear rotates once, the smaller gear rotates twice, so it's twice as fast. It works the other way around, too. A small gear driving a big gear makes the rotation slower.

This gear is upright

This gear is flat

By putting gears at right angles to each other, you can also change the angle of rotation.

# Activity: Follow the Force

Some machines have many interconnecting gearwheels. Look at the machine on this page and see if you can figure out how it works.

If the boy turns the handle clockwise, as shown by the arrow, would the pointer at the end move up, or down?

# Bridge Builders

The very first bridges were very simple—just a log across a small stream. Fast forward to today, though, and we have awesome bridges that cross rivers and ravines.

How did we invent modern bridges like these? How do they stretch across a huge gap, with cars, trucks, and trains driving over them, and still stay up?

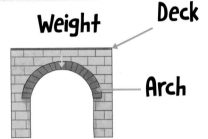

**Weight** · **Deck** · **Arch**

Bridge designers use shapes such as arches to create strong structures.

The Akashi Kaikyo Bridge in Japan has a central single span that stretches 6,532 feet (1,991 m) over the sea.

It is a suspension bridge. The deck is hung, or suspended, from cables attached to tall towers.

Stone, concrete, iron, and steel are strong materials often used in bridges.

Australia's Sydney Harbour Bridge has a single span of 1,650 ft (503 m).

The Sydney Harbour Bridge has a metal arch above the deck. Cables attached to the arch hold the bridge up.

# Activity: Design a Bridge

Find out how bridges stay up, by building some yourself.

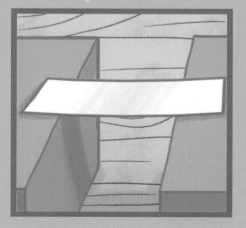

1. Cut a strip of cardboard to make your deck, 12 inches (30 cm) long and 4 inches (10 cm) wide. Use it to make a bridge between the boxes.

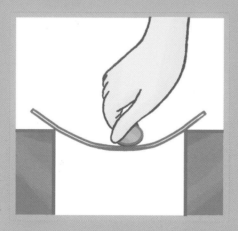

2. Test the bridge by standing the weight in the middle of it. Can a single strip of cardboard hold the weight up?

## You will need:

- thin cardboard, such as a cereal box
- Paper straws
- String
- Scissors
- Pencil and ruler
- Tape
- Two empty cardboard boxes, such as tissue boxes
- An object to use as a test weight, such as an unopened juice box

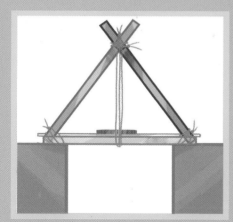

3. If not, use your other materials to try to build a bridge that is strong enough.

You could use cardboard to make an arch to support the deck. Or see if you can build a suspension bridge with straws and string.

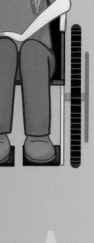

# Hearing Heartbeats

In 1816, René Laennec was a doctor working in Paris, France. In those days, a doctor would listen to a patient's heartbeat by putting his ear against the person's chest or back. One day, he had trouble hearing a patient's heart properly.

Laennec knew that sounds can be heard better when they travel down a tube. He rolled up some paper, held one end against the patient's chest, and put his ear to the other end. It worked! He had invented the stethoscope!

Various people have modified the design of the stethoscope to make it more useful.

1. First, Laennec made a wooden version of his simple paper tube.

2. Later versions had a trumpet-shaped end.

3. British doctor Golding Bird developed this flexible version in 1840.

4. In 1851, Irish doctor Arthur Leared invented a version with earpieces.

5. The stethoscope is a simple but effective tool that is still used today.

# Activity: Cardboard Stethoscope

Make your own stethoscope, and try it out to see if it works.

## You will need:

- A cardboard tube, such as the tube from a roll of paper towel or foil
- A small funnel
- Tape
- A friend!

1. Stick the narrow end of the funnel into one end of the cardboard tube.

2. Tape the tube and the funnel together.

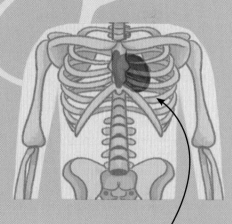

3. Ask a friend or family member if you can try listening to their heartbeat. First try with just your ear, then try using the stethoscope, with the funnel end against the person's chest.

Listen for the heart here.

# Suck It Up!

Vacuum cleaners are an awesomely useful invention. Sucking up dust and crumbs is so much easier than chasing them around with a brush. That's why pretty much every home has one!

The American Daniel Hess probably came up with the idea for the first vacuum cleaner ("carpet sweeper") in 1860. It created suction using hand-pumped bellows.

In 1901, British engineer Hubert Cecil Booth created a vacuum cleaner with a fan driven by an engine. It was so big that it couldn't fit inside a house. Booth visited houses and cleaned them using long, flexible tubes that could reach in through the doors and windows!

The first portable indoor electric vacuum cleaner was invented in 1907. There have been many improvements since then!

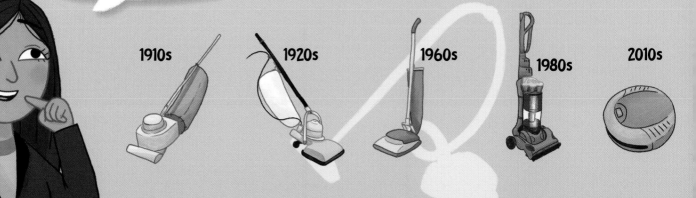

1910s

1920s

1960s

1980s

2010s

# Activity: twisted tubes

The tubes on Hubert Cecil Booth's huge vacuum cleaner have become tangled up.

# Music Machines

Like the wheel, musical instruments are such an old invention that no one knows who first invented them.

The first instruments were probably percussion instruments, such as drums and rattles. People banged sticks and stones together to play a beat. For tunes, inventors had to figure out how tubes, sticks, or strings of different shapes and sizes made different musical notes. The dates given below are approximate.

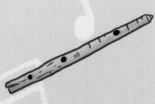

41,000 BCE: The flute is invented. It has holes that you cover with your fingers to blow different notes.

3200 BCE: The first lyre is made. It is a very early stringed instrument.

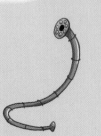

1000 BCE: The lur is invented. It is similar to an early bronze horn.

History is full of amazing musical instrument inventions ...

1709: Italian Bartolomeo Cristofori invents the piano.

1931: The first electric guitar is invented by a group of musicians.

1940s: Hugh Le Caine invents the first electronic synthesizer.

# Activity: Make a Musical Instrument

People still invent musical instruments today, often using everyday objects. Try making this bottle organ to find out how to create different musical notes.

## You will need:

- Some clean, empty glass bottles, preferably the same size
- Water
- A metal spoon

1. First, try playing the bottles. You can tap them with a spoon or blow across the top to make a soft musical note.

2. Stand the bottles in a row, and pour a different amount of water into each one.

3. "Play" the bottles by tapping with a spoon or blowing across the tops to see what notes they make.

4. See if you can adjust the amounts of water to make a musical scale (like on a piano) or a sequence of notes that makes a tune.

# Micro-World

Antonie van Leeuwenhoek was a businessman and self-taught scientist in the Netherlands. In the mid-1600s, he began making magnifying lenses in order to look more closely at tiny living things. Imagine his surprise when he discovered a world of microscopic organisms!

### Antonie van Leeuwenhoek's microscope

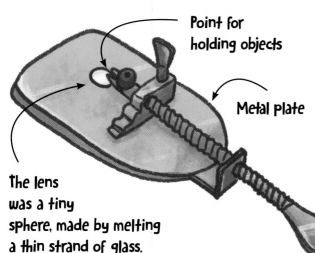

Point for holding objects

Metal plate

The lens was a tiny sphere, made by melting a thin strand of glass.

Van Leeuwenhoek looked at tooth plaque and pond water, among other things. He was amazed to see tiny wriggling creatures, which he called "animalcules."

Now we know that "animalcules" were bacteria and living things.

Drawings of van Leeuwenhoek's "animalcules"

# Activity: Sphere Microscope

You can make a microscope like van Leeuwenhoek's using a drop of water instead of a glass sphere.

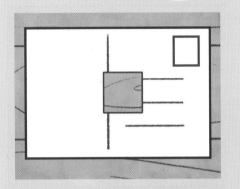

1. Cut a hole in the middle of the card, about 1 inch (2.5 cm) square.

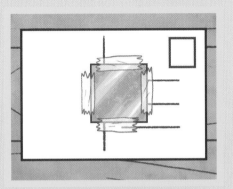

2. Cut a slightly larger piece of foil, and tape it over the hole.

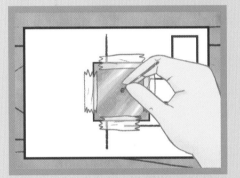

3. Use the needle to make a neat, round hole in the middle of the foil.

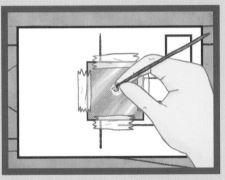

4. Dip the stirrer or skewer in jelly or oil, and dab some around the edge of the hole in the foil.

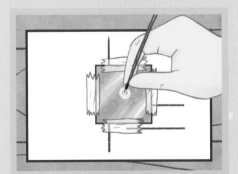

5. Dip the other end of the stirrer or skewer in water, and drop a drop of water onto the hole.

6. Hold the flashlight upright, switch it on, and put the object over the light.

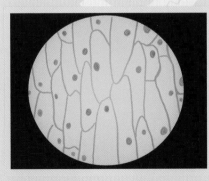

7. Hold the drop of water just above it, and look through the drop as closely as you can with one eye.

# Into Print!

Long ago, when people wanted to make a book, they had to write it out by hand. Specially trained writers called scribes would spend weeks or months carefully writing out each copy.

*There must be a better way than this!*

Around the year 1040, Chinese inventor Bi Sheng made the first movable type using blocks of clay.

Chinese writing uses a symbol for each word, so each block had a word symbol on it. The blocks could be reused.

In the 1440s, German metalworker Johannes Gutenberg invented a printing press. Each type block printed a separate letter. The letters could be rearranged to make words in most European languages.

To print something, printers arranged the type blocks in a frame to make words or sentences. The surface was covered in ink, then pressed onto paper to make a printed page.

# Activity: Block Buster

Printing blocks have to be made as a mirror image of the letter
or word that they print, so that the printed text comes out the correct way.

Can you match all of these Chinese printing blocks to the printed characters they make?

Printing helped spread information to everyone—similar to the internet today.

# X-ray Vision

Have you ever fallen down and think you might have a broken arm? Thanks to the amazing invention of X-ray photos, a doctor can take a look inside your body and see how bad it is.

Like many inventions, X-rays were discovered by accident. In 1895, German scientist Wilhelm Röntgen was experimenting with running electricity through a glass tube. The tube was covered in black paper to keep light from escaping.

But a light-sensitive screen on the other side of the room began to glow, showing that some kind of energy rays were still getting through. Röntgen had no idea what they were, so he called them "X-rays."

X-rays could pass through objects that light could not. When Röntgen put his hand in the way, the rays passed through his flesh but not his bones, making a photo of his skeleton.

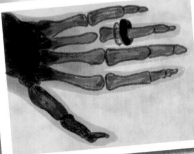

One of Röntgen's first X-rays was his wife's hand. Along with her finger bones, you can see her wedding ring!

X-rays are actually a kind of electromagnetic wave, like light, radio waves, and microwaves.

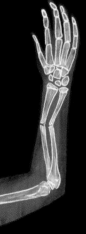

# Activity: Bone Doctor

X-rays are used to take pictures of any part of the skeleton. Can you figure out which bones these X-rays show?

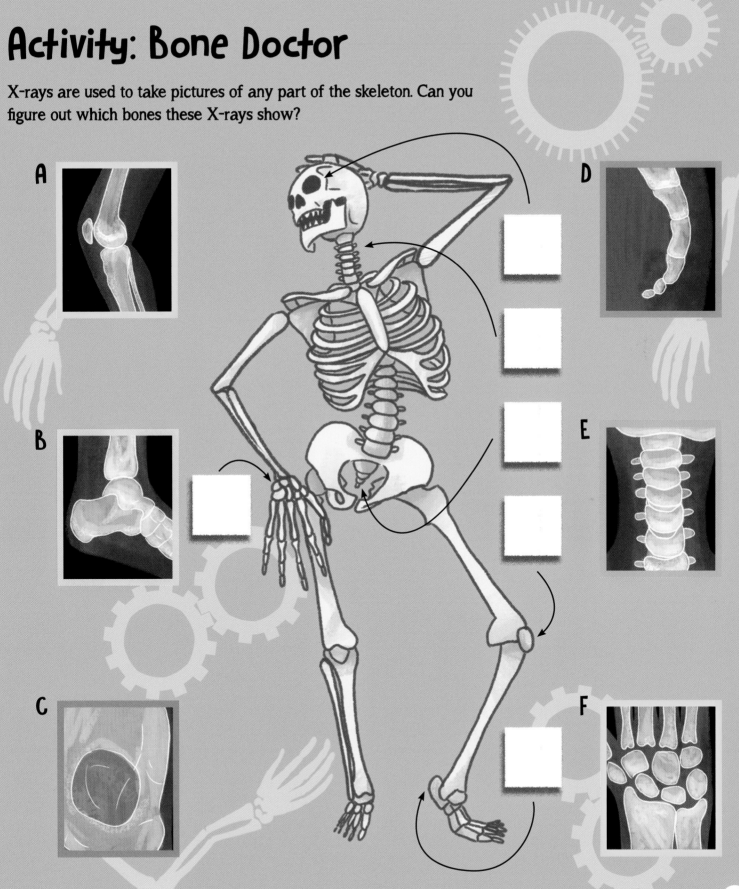

A

B

C

D

E

F

# Gliding on Air

A glider is an unpowered plane. It has no engine—it just glides along on air currents until it finally lands.

For centuries, people have tried to fly by building bird-like wings and trying to flap them. It never worked, because humans aren't light enough or strong enough to fly by flapping.

**875**  Abbas ibn Firnas, an Islamic scientist living in Spain, may have been the first to make a glider flight at the age of 70, using wings made of silk on a wooden frame. He is said to have glided for several minutes.

**1632**  According to legend, Hezârfen Ahmed Çelebi built his own glider wings, to fly across the Bosphorus Strait in Turkey, a distance of about 1 mile (1.5 km).

**1849**  After testing numerous glider designs with no one onboard, British inventor George Cayley launched a glider carrying a passenger (1853).

**1890s**  German engineer Otto Lilienthal built and flew many gliders, making more than 2,000 flights.

**today** Today, people fly gliders as a hobby.

But birds also glide, with their wings spread out. When inventors began trying to fly by gliding instead of flapping, flight took off!

# Activity: Paper Gliders

A paper plane is a type of simple glider.

Try making paper planes that glide as far as possible. You could have a contest with your friends.

1. First, make some basic paper planes. If you're not sure how, follow these diagrams.

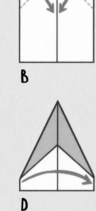

A

B

C

D

E

F

2. Try flying your planes. How far do they glide?

3. Use your inventing skills to improve the planes to make them fly farther. Here are some things you could do:

Cut flaps into the wings and try folding them up or down.

Fold the wing tips up.

Attach tape to add weight to different parts of the plane.

Add an upright tail fin made of paper.

You could even invent a new type of paper plane!

# Flying Machines

Gliders could fly—but not for very long. They had no power, and they were also hard to control. The next step was to build an aircraft based on the glider, but one that had an engine.

Two American brothers, Orville and Wilbur Wright, built the first plane, the Wright Flyer. Its first flight was on December 17, 1903, and lasted only 12 seconds. But the brothers made three more flights that day, and the longest was 59 seconds.

This was the first-ever powered, sustained, steered, and heavier-than-air flight. What does that mean?

It had an engine, which turned propellers to push the plane forward.

The pilot could control the plane's direction and land it safely.

It didn't float like a hot-air balloon.

The plane kept going until the pilot landed it.

# Activity: Spot the Right Wright Flyer!

These two pictures both show the Wright Flyer in action, but they're not quite the same. Only one of these Flyers would actually be able to fly safely.

there are seven differences to spot between the pictures! Can you find them all?

A

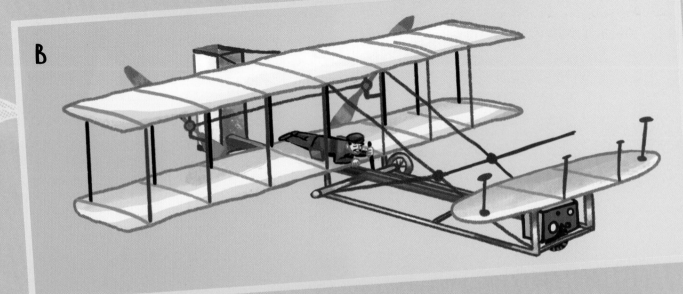

B

27

# Hovering Helicopters

In ancient China, children played with little bamboo spinning toys that could lift up into the air.

To make the toy fly, you rolled the stick between your hands, making the blades rotate.

The two blades were tilted at an angle. If they were spun in the right direction, they pushed air downward as they moved, pushing the toy up.

These toys were the ancestors of the helicopter, which works the same way.

A helicopter can take off and land vertically, or it can hover in the air.

As the rotors spin around in a circle, they push air down, and this pushes the helicopter up.

Helicopters can do things that planes can't, such as landing on a mountain or rescuing people from the sea.

# Helicopter timeline

1905

1907

1922

# Activity: Make a Spinning Helicopter

The ancient Chinese toy was made of bamboo, but you can easily make your own version from card and a wooden skewer.

1. Measure and cut a piece of cardboard about 8 inches (20 cm) by 1 inch (2.5 cm).

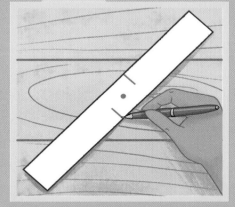

2. Mark the cardboard in the middle with a dot and two lines, like this.

5. To fly the helicopter, hold the stick between your hands and roll it to make the blades spin—then let go.

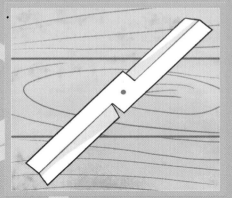

3. Cut along the lines, and fold the opposite edges of the cardboard downward, like this.

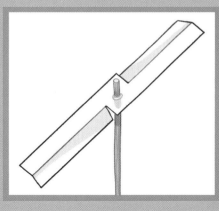

4. Stick the skewer upward through the dot, with a little glue to attach it. Cut off the sharp end.

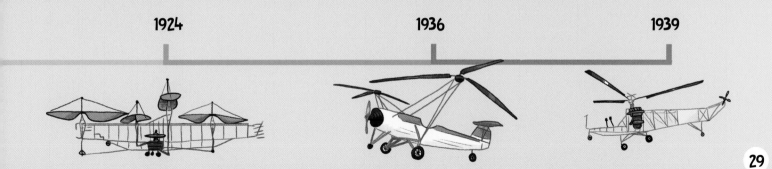

1924        1936        1939

29

# Maglev Trains

If you've ever played with two magnets, you will have felt the attraction (pulling force) when you hold them close to each other. But if you turn one of them around, they push each other apart instead.

Around 1900, inventors realized that this magnetic repulsion could be used to hold a train up in the air. Instead of using wheels, which rub against the track and cause friction, the train would float along on a magnetic "cushion." This idea became known as a maglev train, short for "magnetic levitation."

Magnets have two opposite poles—usually the opposite ends or sides of the magnet. If you put two opposite poles together, they attract, or pull.

But if you put two like poles together, they push apart. It feels like an invisible bouncy cushion between the magnets.

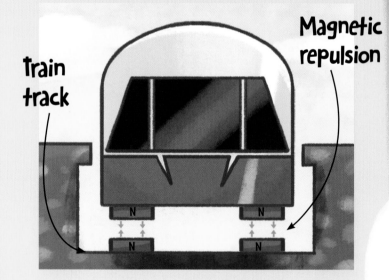

**Train track**

**Magnetic repulsion**

China's Shanghai Maglev is the fastest passenger train in the world. It runs up to 268 mph (431 km/h).

# Activity: Model Maglev

How would you make a model maglev train? Imagine you had the materials below, and draw a design to show how you could make a cardboard maglev train run along a magnetic track.

Remember, the train can't just balance on top of the track—it will slide off. It needs some kind of channel to fit into, as in the diagram opposite.

Cardboard boxes

Thick cardboard
Glue
Tape

Flat coin magnets

If you have the right materials, you could try building your model, too!

# Dot Dot Dot, Dash Dash

Today, you can send a message to someone in another country instantly. But 200 years ago, messages had to travel by foot, horse, carriage, or boat, and they could take weeks or months to arrive.

The telegraph was invented in the 1830s. A long electric circuit was set up, linking two places. Connecting the circuit at one end made electricity flow. This made a buzzer or light work at the other end, so it sent an almost-instant signal.

## International Morse Code

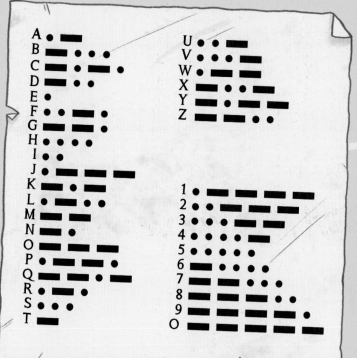

So you could send a signal—but how could you turn that into a message, made up of words and sentences? Americans Samuel Morse and Alfred Vail came up with a code made up of "dashes and dots," or long and short signals. It was called Morse code.

Vail also built a machine that recorded the dots and dashes on a piece of moving tape. To read the message, you collected the tape, decoded the dashes and dots, and wrote down the letters. You can see the first ever Morse code message here.

WHAT HATH GOD WROUGHT

# Activity: Decode the Code

Samuel Morse first tested his system in 1838. Before long, telegraph lines were carrying messages in Morse code all around the world.

Can you decode these Morse messages? Use the Morse code chart opposite to help you.

**1**

- .... . / . - - .-. . / ...- .- .-. .. . ... / ..- - -/

_ _ _ _ / _ _ _ _ _ _ / _ _ _ _ _ _ / _ _ _ /

-- .. -.. -- .. --- .... -

_ _ _ _ _ _ _ _

**2**

.. -- / -.-. --- -- -- .. -. --. / - --- / .... .. ... .. - /

_ _ _ / _ _ _ _ _ _ _ / _ _ / _ _ _ _ _ _ _ /

.... --- .-.. . / .. - .-. .. . / -- .. -.-. ....

_ _ _ _ / _ _ _ _ _ _ / _ _ _ _ _

**3**

--- . . - / -- . / --- - -. / - .- .... . / .-.- --- -.. -.. . . . .-. /

_ _ _ _ / _ _ / _ _ / _ _ _ / _ _ _ _ _ /

.... .... . .---- .-.-.- - .... / ... .- .-. . . . .

_ _ / _ _ _ _ / _ _ _ _ _ _

33

# Sound Recording

We can listen to music whenever we like, because we can record it, store it, and play it back. Thanks to sound recording, we can also watch movies and TV with sound, listen to audiobooks, and leave phone messages.

When objects make contact, they vibrate. This makes the air around them vibrate, too. Our ears detect the vibrations, and that's how we hear. To record sound, you have to find a way of capturing the pattern of vibrations.

French printer Édouard-Léon Scott de Martinville invented the "phonautograph" in 1857.

Sound vibrations were picked up by the cone and made the needle vibrate.

The needle left a pattern in the soot on the cylinder.

The phonautograph recorded sound, but there was no way to play it back.

**Since then, we've invented many more ways to record sound ...**

The "phonograph" was similar to the phonautograph, but instead of soot, Thomas Edison covered the cylinder in tin foil. It was created in 1877 by American inventor Thomas Edison.

1. The needle scratched a groove in the foil containing vibration patterns.

2. Another needle would run through the groove, making the needle vibrate ...

3. ... and this caused another vibration, making a sound that could be heard.

The first thing Edison recorded was the first line of the nursery rhyme "Mary Had a Little Lamb."

Vinyl record

Cassette tape

CD

MP3

# Activity: Waveforms

Besides recording sounds, a computer can show the pattern of sound vibrations as a waveform graph, like this:

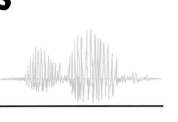

Can you match each sound to the waveform it makes?

## 1. Flushing toilet    2. ticking clock    3. Ocean waves    4. Ringing bell

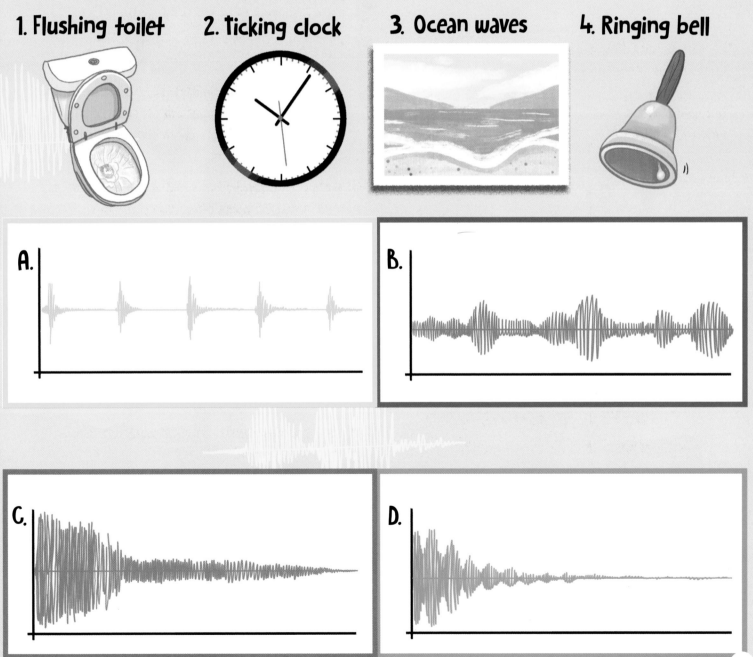

A.

B.

C.

D.

# Can You Hear Me?

When telephones were invented, people could have long-distance conversations. But before the telephone, there was another way of doing this. It couldn't carry voices as far as a telephone, but it was still really useful. It was the speaking tube.

**Giambattista della Porta**

**Jean-Baptiste Biot**

In the 1500s, Italian scientist Giambattista della Porta wrote that the sound of speech could travel "hundreds of paces" along a lead tube.

In the early 1800s, French scientist Jean-Baptiste Biot experimented with the water pipes of Paris. He found they could carry a voice 1,040 yards (950 m).

In the nineteenth century, speaking tubes were used in big houses, so that people could give instructions to their servants.

Before phones, ships used speaking tubes to link the bridge to the boiler room and other remote areas.

Speaking tubes are still used today! They can sometimes be found in playgrounds.

# Activity: tube talking

Make your own speaking tube to link two different rooms or floors in your house or school. You could also create a tube from a garden hose or lots of long cardboard tubes taped together.

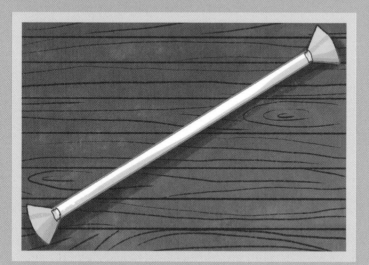

1. Stick the funnels into the two ends of the tubes, and use tape to hold them in place.

2. Arrange the tube so that one end is in one room and one end is in another.

3. Use cable ties or string to hold the tube in place by tying it to fixed objects, such as coat hooks or handrails.

4. Try using the tube. If you speak into one end, even quietly, another person should be able to hear you clearly at the other end.

# Light in a Box

Around the year 1000, the Arab scientist Ibn al-Haytham (also known as Alhazen) was experimenting with light. He made a dark box with a tiny hole, or "pinhole," in one wall and a row of candles outside it. He found that images of the candles appeared on the opposite wall inside the box—but upside down and back to front.

Ibn al-Haytham also figured out that our eyes work the same way.

Each eyeball is like a mini camera obscura.

The pupil works as the pinhole.

An upside-down image forms on the back of the eye.

When the signals reach your brain, it turns the image the right way up. That's why you don't see everything upside down!

This is called a camera obscura, meaning "dark chamber." Ibn al-Haytham realized that light moved in straight lines, or rays, and that each ray shining through the tiny hole ended up on the opposite side from where it had started.

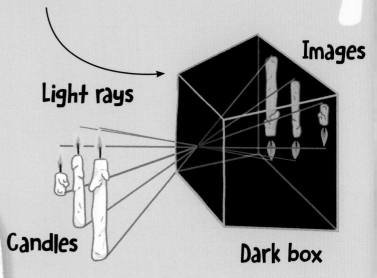

Light rays

Images

Candles

Dark box

In the 1800s, photographic cameras worked this way, too. The image was projected onto light-sensitive film or plates to make a photo.

# Activity: Alhazen's Image

This camera obscura is pointing at a view of a city. Can you draw the upside-down, back-to-front picture that will appear inside it?

You can make your own camera obscura! Choose a sunny day, and make your room very dark. Open a tiny gap in the curtains or blinds, and you should see a reversed image of the view outside appear on the opposite wall!

# Hovercraft

A hovercraft is a vehicle that can travel over both land and water, and it has no wheels. It works by pushing air downward, making an air "cushion" that it floats on.

The idea of the hovercraft has been around for hundreds of years, but the first successful, working hovercraft was invented in the 1950s by a British engineer, Christopher Cockerell. He cobbled together everyday items to make a prototype model.

Cockerell used a large cat food can with a slightly smaller coffee can inside it.

He blew air through a hole in the top of the outer can using a hairdryer.

SR.N1

This made a downward-moving curtain of air around the edge, which lifted the cans up.

After that, Cockerell made bigger models, and finally the SR.N1, the first full-sized, long-distance hovercraft.

Hovercraft are now used around the world. This hovercraft glides off the coast of India.

# Activity: Hovercraft Model

This simple model works a bit like a real hovercraft.

## You will need:

- An old, unwanted CD or DVD (try a secondhand store if you don't have one already)
- A spout-style top from a water bottle
- Strong glue
- A balloon

The air blowing through and under the CD makes a cushion, and the model can glide along easily.

1. If the bottle spout has a lid, pull it off. Make sure the spout is open and air can blow through it.

2. Glue the spout over the hole in the middle of the CD, making sure there are no gaps.

3. Blow up the balloon, and hold it closed. Fit the neck of the balloon over the spout. Put the hovercraft on a flat, smooth surface, and let go.

# Spectacles

We often think of the human body as an amazing thing—and it is. But it's not perfect. Things often go wrong, and one thing that often goes wrong is our eyesight.

Before spectacles, people used a reading stone. This was actually a piece of glass that was flat on one side and curved on the other.

Eyeglasses appeared in Italy about 1290. The first glasses were made by putting two reading stones into a frame.

The reading stone magnified text, making it easier for people with poor eyesight to see.

By the 1350s, portraits started showing people wearing glasses, like this one of Cardinal Hugo of Provence.

And by about 1400, lens makers had discovered how to make different types of glasses to solve different problems.

Around 16% of human beings have serious eye problems, and more than half of us need glasses!

Eyes working perfectly focus an image on the retina at the back of the eye.

Near-sighted eyes focus the image before the retina.

Far-sighted eyes focus the image behind the retina.

The lenses of glasses bend the light to focus it in the right place.

Retina

# Activity: Eyeglasses timeline

People have been coming up with eyesight improvement ideas since ancient times. Can you put these inventions in the right order along the timeline?

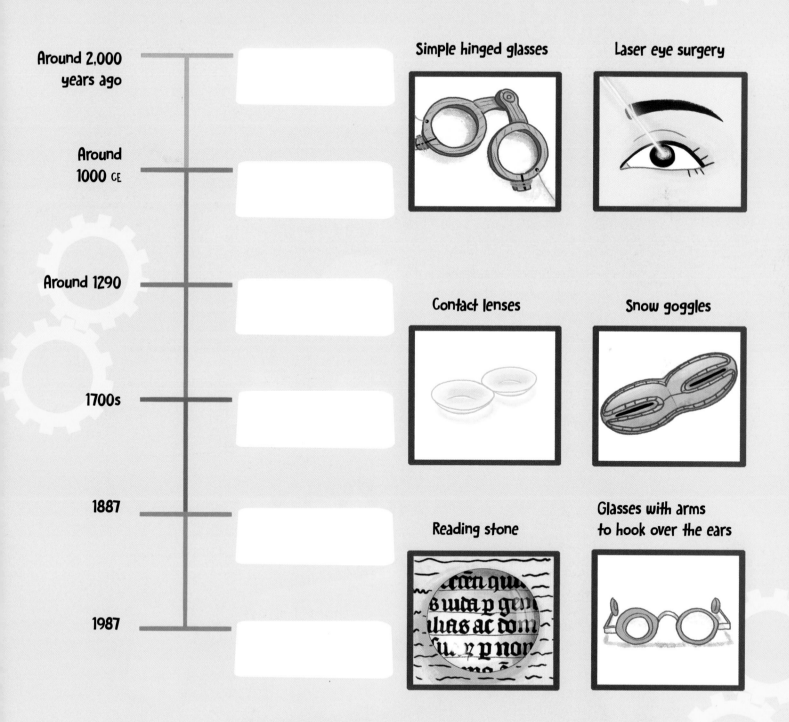

Around 2,000 years ago

Around 1000 CE

Around 1290

1700s

1887

1987

Simple hinged glasses

Laser eye surgery

Contact lenses

Snow goggles

Reading stone

Glasses with arms to hook over the ears

# Computer Mouse

In the early days of computing, you operated a computer by typing special instructions into it, called command lines. Most people didn't know these command lines, so only computer experts could use computers.

In the 1960s, computer engineer Douglas Engelbart was working on ways to make computers easier for everyone to use.

He came up with this idea, which he called the "X-Y position indicator for a display system."

**Wire**

It was made of wood, with a wire to connect it to the computer.

**Wheels**

Inside were two wheels that rolled to and fro as you moved the indicator around on a desk.

The device was nicknamed the "mouse" (because its cord looked like a tail)—and the name stuck.

The mouse led to other interactive systems, such as touchpads and touchscreens.

The mouse changed computing. Instead of command lines, the Graphical User Interface (or GUI) took over. People could use the mouse to select icons, menus, and other options on the screen. This paved the way for computers that everyone could use at home.

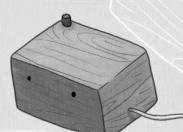

# Activity: Where on the Screen?

Engelbart's mouse worked by dividing the screen into a grid with X (left to right) and Y (up and down) lines.

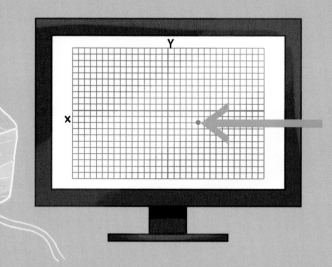

Moving the mouse tells the computer to move the cursor from one part of the grid to another. For example, the dot on this screen is at X = 5 / Y = –2

Use these coordinates to mark mouse cursor points on this screen. What picture do they make?

X = 5  /  Y = –2
X = 4  /  Y = –3
X = 2  /  Y = –4
X = 0  /  Y = –4
X = –2 /  Y = –4
X = –4 /  Y = –3
X = –5 /  Y = –2
X = 0  /  Y = 0
X = 5  /  Y = 4
X = 5  /  Y = –4

# Programming Language

Computers need instructions, or software, to make them work, and software is written in special programming languages.

Charles Babbage designed a computing machine in the 1830s called the Difference Engine. It was designed to perform calculations. He later developed the Analytical Engine.

Ada Lovelace worked with Babbage. She realized that punched cards could feed instructions into the Analytical Engine. This idea was an early computer program.

Babbage and Lovelace never managed to make a finished working computer, but they laid the foundations for others to work on.

Punched instruction cards

the Analytical Engine

A programming language called BASIC

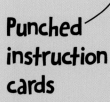

110   IF (N < 20) THEN GOTO 50

In the 1940s and 1950s, electronic computers were invented. Computers store and calculate information using binary code, which is made up of only 0s and 1s.

This is very hard for humans to work with—so we need a programming language. This is a way to write computer software so that it makes more sense to us.

# Activity: Program a Friend

Programming languages work by using lines of code. Each line gives a simple instruction. Here's a very small, simple example:

1. CLS ⟶ clears the screen
2. Print "Hello!" ⟶ prints "Hello!" on the screen
3. End ⟶ end of program

Try inventing your own programming language and write a simple program to make a friend perform an activity, such as going into another room to fetch something.

Your instructions might look something like this:
1. Stand up
2. Turn to the right
3. Take 5 steps forward ...

**Bang!!!**

According to old accounts, people in China began mixing chemicals to try to create potions that would allow them to live forever. They didn't succeed, but they did create something else—fireworks!

Around 1,200 years ago, Chinese experimenters found that certain chemical mixtures would explode when a flame touched them.

They realized that if they put the powder in a bamboo or paper tube, then set it on fire, it would shoot out and explode with a bang and a bright light.

Fireworks technology soon spread around the world. People began experimenting and mixing in other chemicals. Adding copper, for example, will make blue explosions.

Fireworks are still popular today at celebrations such as weddings, festivals, the Fourth of July, and New Year's Eve.

# Activity: Cool Fireworks

One problem with fireworks is that they are hot and explosive, and therefore can be dangerous. So instead of making real fireworks, experiment with designing and making your own cool indoor fireworks display.

## You will need:

- Scissors
- Tape
- Tissue paper
- Sequins
- A toilet paper tube
- A balloon
- Bending straws
- Paper

## To make a straw rocket:

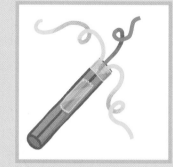

1. Wrap a small piece of paper around a bending straw, and tape it in place to make a tube slightly wider than the straw.

2. Bend the end over and tape it closed. Cut thin strips of tissue paper and tape them to the closed end.

3. Fit the rocket over the long end of the bending straw, and blow hard into the other end.

## To make an exploding firework:

1. Tie the end of the balloon closed (without blowing it up), and cut the top part off.

2. Stretch the bottom end of the balloon over one end of the toilet paper tube, and tape it in place.

3. Put tiny pieces of tissue paper or sequins into the top of the tube. Holding it firmly, pull the bottom of the balloon down, then let go.

# Compass

North, south, east, or west? If you want to know which way you're going, you need a compass. A compass doesn't need any electricity to work—it's just a magnetic needle. As long as it can move freely, the needle will always line itself up north to south.

Compasses were invented in ancient China and date back around 2,000 years. The first ones were made using lodestone, a type of natural magnetic rock.

This early compass is made of a lodestone spoon, shaped so that it can balance and rotate itself easily. The handle always points south, so it was called a "south-pointer."

At first, the ancient Chinese mainly used compasses for planning where to build things. But over time, sailors began using compasses to find their way at sea, and they developed many new designs.

If you float a plastic lid in a bowl of water and put a bar magnet on it, you'll see it turn to point north-south.

Compasses work because Earth itself is a very large magnet and has north and south magnetic poles. These are very close to the North and South Poles that Earth spins around.

**North Pole**

**South Pole**

# Activity: Navigate to the Treasure

There's a treasure chest buried on one of these islands—but where? Set off from the flag at Pirateport and follow the compass directions, using a ruler to measure the distances.

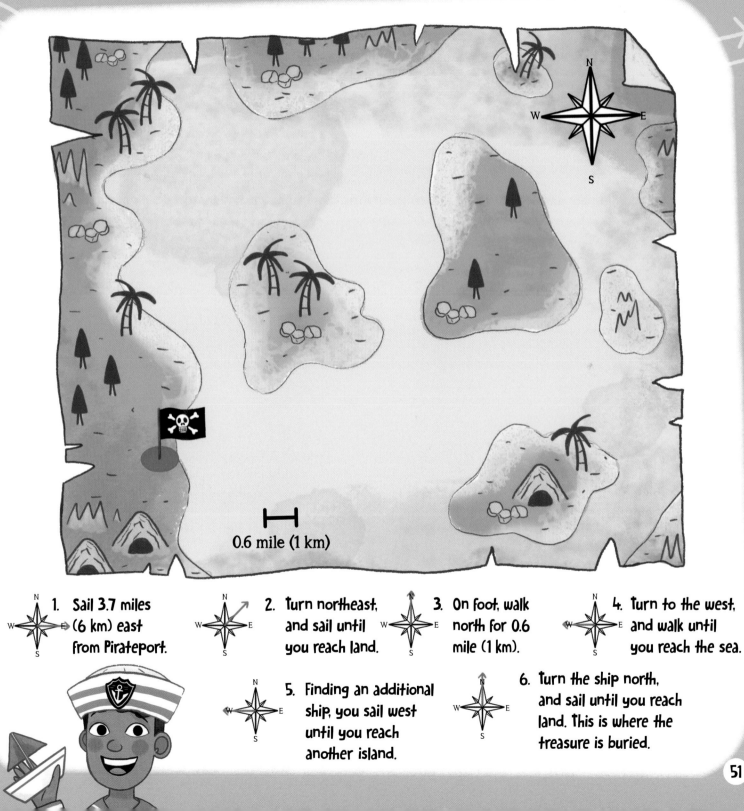

0.6 mile (1 km)

1. Sail 3.7 miles (6 km) east from Pirateport.

2. Turn northeast, and sail until you reach land.

3. On foot, walk north for 0.6 mile (1 km).

4. Turn to the west, and walk until you reach the sea.

5. Finding an additional ship, you sail west until you reach another island.

6. Turn the ship north, and sail until you reach land. This is where the treasure is buried.

# The Earth Is Shaking!

Before a big earthquake, there are often smaller tremors or "foreshocks." Detecting them can save lives.

As long ago as 132 CE, Chinese scientist Zhang Heng invented an early seismoscope, or quake detector. It was a large jar surrounded by bronze dragons with balls in their mouths. When the Earth shook, the dragons' mouths opened and dropped the balls.

Later seismoscopes used a heavy pendulum to detect shaking movements. This one, invented by Italian Andrea Bina in 1751, has a weight hanging on a string, with a pointer below it touching a tray of sand.

When the earth shakes, the pendulum moves and makes marks in the sand.

The wider the pattern of marks, the bigger the tremor.

In the 1800s, geologists developed seismographs—quake detectors that could draw a line on a moving piece of paper. They could now record tremors.

This is a seismograph record of a huge earthquake that hit Japan in 2011.

# Activity: Model Seismoscope

Make your own model to see how a pendulum seismoscope works. You'll need a friend for this experiment—to be your earthquake!

1. Make a hole in the bottom of the cup, and push the pen through so it points downward.

2. Half-fill the cup with coins, pebbles, or marbles to make it heavier and hold the pen in place.

3. Cut a long piece of string and tape the ends to the sides of the cup.

4. Stand the box on its side and make a hole in the top. Thread the middle of the string through the hole.

5. Tape the string in place, so that the pen hangs just above the bottom of the box.

6. Cut two slots in the sides of the box at the same level as the pen tip. Feed a long strip of paper through, so that the pen touches it.

## You will need:

- A large cardboard box
- String
- Scissors
- Tape
- A paper cup
- Coins, pebbles, or marbles
- A marker pen
- A long strip of paper
- A friend!

Ask your friend to gently shake the table while you pull the paper through the box.

# Clever Levers

A lever is a very simple machine. People have been using levers since ancient times, and they're an important part of many great inventions.

A lever is basically a stick that pivots around a point called a fulcrum.

A seesaw is an example of a basic lever.

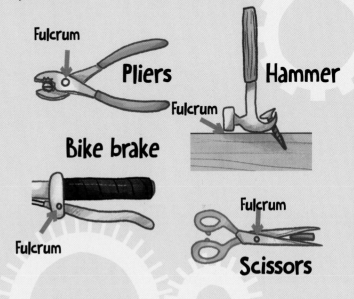

When one end moves up, the other end moves down.

This is the fulcrum, where the lever pivots.

the long part is the lever.

Levers are very useful because they can give you extra power for doing a job. For example, when you use a spoon handle to get the lid off a container, you're using a lever.

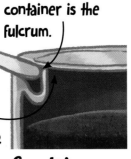

**Spoon**

You push down the long end of the spoon.

The edge of the container is the fulcrum.

The short end pushes the lid up.

**Container**

Because the fulcrum is near one end, the long end moves farther than the short end. But they still both have the same amount of energy, so the short end pushes harder to get the lid off.

Loads of everyday inventions use levers. Here are just a few:

Fulcrum

**Pliers**

**Hammer**

Fulcrum

**Bike brake**

Fulcrum

Fulcrum

**Scissors**

# Activity: Lever Ballistics

Another use of levers was in catapults that fired rocks at castles in medieval times.

## You will need:

- A large wooden or plastic spoon
- A pencil
- A cardboard box narrower than the pencil
- Scissors
- Tape
- Rubber bands
- Paper clip
- Small, light missiles, such as cotton balls, marshmallows, or scrunched-up newspaper

1. Use several rubber bands to fix the spoon across the pencil, like this. Tie one end of a rubber band to the handle end of the spoon.

2. Cut one end off the box. Make holes in the sides of the box, near the top, and push the ends of the pencil through them. Now make a hole in the bottom of the box, below the spoon handle.

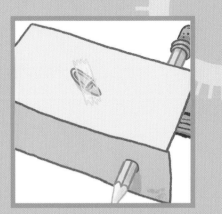

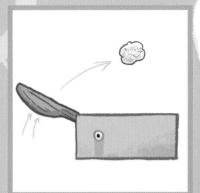

3. Push the other end of the rubber band through the hole. Secure it on the other side with a paper clip and tape.

4. Now try firing your catapult. Push the spoon back, and place a missile on it. Now let go!

This simple model really works! Can you fire your missiles at a target? How accurate is your catapult?

# New Body Parts

A prosthetic is an artificial replacement for a missing body part, such as an arm or leg.

Prosthetics date back to ancient times. They were especially important in times of war, when many people lost limbs.

When Roman general Marcus Sergius lost a hand in battle, he had an iron hand made. It could hold his shield and allowed him to return to fighting.

In 1566, astronomer Tycho Brahe lost his nose in a duel and got a metal replacement.

More recently, we've invented prosthetics that can move and work like the body part they replace.

One way to do this is to use strings that pull on parts to make them bend. This is actually what happens in the real human body, too.

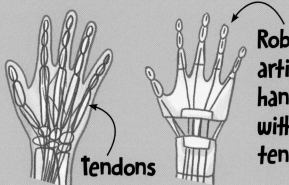

Tendons

Robot artificial hand with cord tendons

In a real hand, strings called tendons pull on the fingers to bend and straighten them.

The sixteenth-century pirate Francois le Clerc was known to his enemies as "Pie de Palo," or "Stick Leg."

# Activity: Moving finger

Make a bending model finger.

## You will need:

- A straw
- String
- Scissors
- Tape

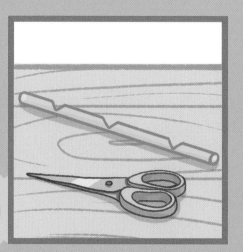

1. Use the scissors to cut three triangle-shaped notches along one side of the straw about 1 inch (2.5 cm) apart.

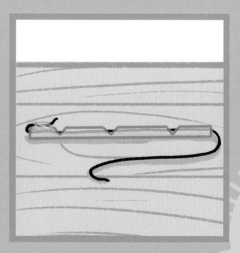

2. Cut a piece of string about 2 inches (5 cm) longer than your straw. Thread it through the straw.

Modern mechanical arm

3. Tape the string to the top end of the straw to hold it in place. To bend the finger, hold it at the base and pull the string.

Can you use the same technology to make other things? How about:
- A hand with 4 fingers and a thumb?
- A working foot?
- An octopus?

57

# Pop Quiz

Have you been paying attention? Test your knowledge of the world's wonderful inventions here! Write your answers on page 59. The answers are on page 61.

1. Put these inventions in the order they were invented.

   Microscope
   Hovercraft
   Spectacles
   Electric guitar
   Computer mouse
   Printing press

2. If the red wheel revolves 10 times every minute, how fast will the green wheel move? Will it revolve 5 times every minute or 20 times every minute?

3. What was this invention used for?

4. True or false? Before the microscope, people did not know about bacteria.

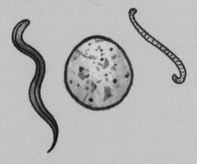

5. How did X-rays get their name?

   A) Their inventor was named Ray Xavier.
   B) They were so mysterious that their inventor. didn't know what else to call them.
   C) The first time they were seen, they formed an "X" shape on the wall.

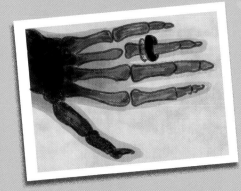

6. What makes a plane different from a bamboo spinning toy? Fill in the chart about flight opposite. The first one has been done for you.

7. Magnets can attract or repulse each other. Which force do maglev trains use?

8. To make these pliers stonger, would you make the handles longer or shorter?

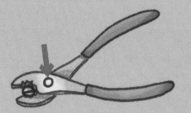

9. True or false? Earthquake tremors could not be predicted until the invention of electricity.

10. If you wanted to make a compass, what items would you need from this list?

A) map
B) bar magnet
C) pendulum
D) bowl of water
E) lid that can float on water
F) cardboard box
G) sunlight

Write down your answers here, and check them on page 61.

1. ..........................................................................

2. ..........................................................................

3. ..........................................................................

4. ..........................................................................

5. ..........................................................................

6. ..........................................................................

|  | Heavier than air | Steered | Powered | Sustained |
|---|---|---|---|---|
| Plane | X | X | X | X |
| Bamboo spinning toy |  |  |  |  |
| Modern glider |  |  |  |  |
| Helicopter |  |  |  |  |

7. ..........................................................................

8. ..........................................................................

9. ..........................................................................

10. ..........................................................................

# Answers

**P. 21**

1 = C
2 = E
3 = A
4 = B
5 = D

**P. 23**

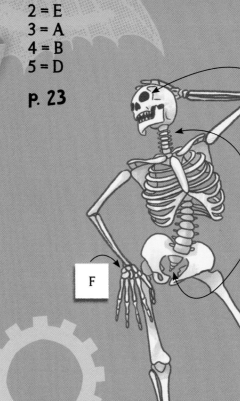

**P. 7**   The pictures should go in this order:

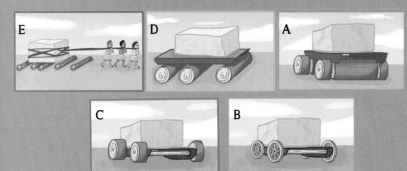

**P. 9**   The last cog would move clockwise, so the pointer would move down.

**P. 15**

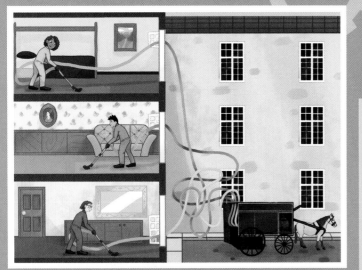

Tube A–Boy in green       Tube C–Girl in red
Tube B–Girl in yellow

**P. 27**

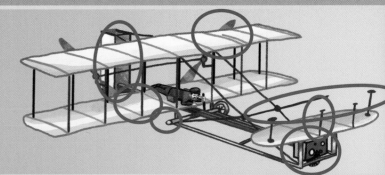

## P. 33

1 = THE EAGLE FLIES AT MIDNIGHT

2 = I'M COMING TO VISIT LOVE AUNTIE MAUD

3 = MEET ME ON THE CORNER OF 12TH STREET

## P. 35

A = 2
B = 3
C = 1
D = 4

## P. 43

Around 2,000 years ago = snow goggles
Around 1000 CE = reading stone
Around 1290 = simple hinged glasses
1700s = glasses with arms to hook over the ears
1887 = contact lenses
1987 = laser eye surgery

## P. 45

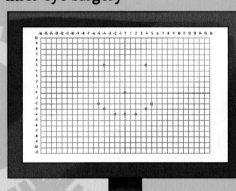

## P. 51

## PP. 58–59

1. Spectacles 1290s
   Printing press 1440s
   Microscope 1670s
   Electric guitar 1930s
   Hovercraft 1950s
   Computer mouse 1960s

2. The green wheel will revolve 5 times.

3. It was an early stethoscope, used for listening to heartbeats.

4. True.

5. B

6.

| | Heavier than air | Steered | Powered | Sustained |
|---|---|---|---|---|
| Plane | X | X | X | X |
| Bamboo spinning toy | X | | | |
| Modern glider | X | X | | X |
| Helicopter | X | X | X | X |

7. Repulse.

8. Longer.

9. False.

10. You would need b, d, and e. Place the bar magnet on the lid, and float it on a bowl of water. The magnet will turn to point to magnetic north.

# Glossary

**Air current**  A body of air moving in a definite direction.

**Axle**  A fixed or rotating rod that passes through the middle of a wheel.

**Bacteria**  A large group of single-cell microorganisms, some of which cause diseases.

**Binary**  The counting system that uses only two numbers, 0 and 1.

**Cable**  A thick rope used for holding up a bridge, often made of steel.

**Chemical**  Any basic substance that is used in (or produced by) a reaction involving changes to atoms or molecules.

**Cog**  A wheel with a series of teeth on its edge that transfers motion by linking with another cog.

**Compass**  An instrument for finding directions. It consists of a magnetized pointer that always points north.

**Electromagnetic wave**  A wave of energy that can travel through a vacuum at the speed of light. Includes radio waves, infrared, visible light, ultraviolet, X-rays, and gamma rays.

**Force**  An influence that produces a physical change or a change in movement.

**Fulcrum**  The point on which a bar or other lever is supported.

**Gear**  A device, often made of connecting wheels with teeth, that alters the relation between the speed of an engine and other moving parts.

**GUI (Graphical User Interface)**  A computer program designed to allow a user to interact easily with the computer.

**Hover**  To stay in one place in the air.

**Lens**  A piece of glass with one or both sides curved for concentrating or dispersing light rays.

**Machine**  A piece of equipment with several moving parts. It uses power to do a particular type of work.

**Magnetic**  Attracting iron or steel.

**Magnify**  To make something appear bigger than it is, usually with a lens or microscope.

**Medieval**  From the Middle Ages (the period in European history from around 600–1500 CE).

**Microorganism**  A living creature that is too small for us to see with the naked eye.

**Mirror image**  An identical image but reversed, as if seen in a mirror.

**Movable type**  An individual word, letter, or punctuation mark placed in a frame to be used for printing. They are movable because they can be taken out and reused for the next batch of printing.

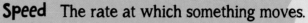

**Pendulum**   A weight hung from a fixed point so it can swing freely.

**Percussion instrument**   Musical instrument played by shaking or hitting (with a stick or the hand).

**Pivot**   Movement around a central point.

**Pole**   The end of a magnet, north or south, where the magnetic force is strongest.

**Portable**   Small or light enough to be carried or moved easily.

**Prehistoric**   From the time before written history.

**Ray**   A narrow stream of energy, usually of visible light, moving in a straight line.

**Retina**   A layer at the back of the eyeball that contains light-sensitive cells.

**Rotation**   Movement around a central point or axis.

**Rotor**   A part of a machine that spins, especially the part supporting the turning blades that provide lift for a helicopter.

**Scribe**   A person whose job was to write, particularly to copy documents.

**Seismograph**   An instrument that measures and records details of motion in the ground, such as earthquakes and volcanic eruptions.

**Seismoscope**   An instrument that responds to motion in the ground, such as earthquakes and volcanic eruptions.

**Single-celled**   One of the tiny units from which all living things are made.

**Span**   The length of something from point to point; the distance on a bridge between two supports.

**Speed**   The rate at which something moves.

**Spoke**   A rod connecting the outer edge of a wheel to its midpoint.

**Stethoscope**   A medical instrument for listening to a person's heart or breathing.

**Suction**   The removal of air to create a partial vacuum.

**Suspension bridge**   A bridge where the weight of the deck is supported by vertical cables attached to other cables that run between towers.

**Technology**   The use of scientific knowledge to develop machinery and equipment.

**Tendon**   A tough tissue that connects a muscle to a bone.

**Tool**   An item used to help perform a job.

**Tremor**   A wobbling, quivering movement in the ground, especially following earthquakes and volcanic eruptions.

**Vibration**   Continuous, regular shaking movement.

**Wheel**   A circular object that revolves on an axle and forms part of a machine.

# Index